Where a road had been

Matt Shears

BlazeVOX [books]

Buffalo, New York

Where a road had been by Matt Shears

Copyright © 2010

Published by BlazeVOX [books]

Printed in the United States of America

Book design by Geoffrey Gatza

Cover photo by Rayhannah Dar

First Edition
ISBN: 978-1-60964-048-4
Library of Congress Control Number 2009910029

BlazeVOX [books]
303 Bedford Ave
Buffalo, NY 14216

Editor@blazevox.org

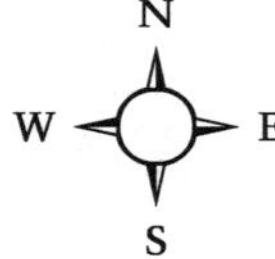

publisher of weird little books

BlazeVOX [books]

blazevox.org

2   4   6   8   0   9   7   5   3   1

B   X

Acknowledgments

The author gratefully acknowledges teachers, friends and family who helped this book come about. Sections of "Where a road had been" first appeared in Alice Blue Review, BlazeVox and Cricket Online Review. "A Market," "A Wholeness, I answered," "An Ecosystem," and "A Social Poem" appeared in the September/October 2007 Poets Sampler of Boston Review (introduced by Claudia Keelan.) "A fascination" appeared in The Argotist Online. "A position" appeared in Cutbank. "A next" appeared in Denver Quarterly. "An else," and "An oversight" appeared in Diner. "Among the fields" appeared in MiPOesias, originally as "perpetual I of its erasure." "A darkness, I answered" appeared in Marginalia. "A sighting," and "A river, a little town" appeared in Notre Dame Review. Sincere thanks are extended to all of the editors and their staffs. Thanks also to Adrienne Deaton for her wise and patient council. And finally, a hearty thanks to Geoffrey Gatza and BlazeVOX books!

Contents

Where a road had been

New garden

a next

what becomes lost, an i wishes
permanence upon, where you could
not leave it, where it wasn't,
it speaks, there is no death, nature
couldn't argue, any differently.

they became absences, it seemed
when it folded up, when did it close,
we weren't certainly, upon a table
in a voicelessness, the duration
felt along the edges, was i there

at all. later the still-framed rose,
something flying, through the window,
sight carried little, i thought
of hammers, and other disasters
rose and began, to separate quickly.

a position

their closure began   with beginnings
an opening   lying supine

the table somewhat   incomplete

how   the disaster did not
carry its weight   away how the light

sought itself   moving against every

position   the hole swallowed
a boundary   of small stars   strung

along a beach   the wind severed

*

its persistence   a tide receding
from intention,   direction

its unsequenced   'story'

a shimmering non-entity   a cloud
where they moved   into futures

of grief   a ground hollowed
out   a foundation   which damaged

a mouth caught   in its flickering

                          *

elevation   clearing into song
without morning   one dreamed

the edges of sound   coming apart

outlines, shorelines   in mist lifting
away promises   impelled always

the use of force   the resistance

it fed upon   a space filled with
no earth   its earth   without sky

an else

the fever   through eras, burnt
eyelids away   from a sun

unseen   in that picture   held
to its ground   a reason one

furthered, a bridge through   the city
spread every   laminate toward

an edge   unsolid   they spoke
of desire   and why we—

echoing a cavernous   progression
they dream only   of ending

*

to the fever, the fervor   a cell
clung to   the rooftops   a light

stuck   in eternity   the infinite
model scaffolding   smaller and

smaller windows   a breach
of ors, the irises   dropping away

a reinvention of self   in street
it could not be   written, only

the motion of moving   toward it
how opposition   has its pluses

an ecosystem

its consolation,   embedded mimicries
one noticed   (a further spring, a rose, a moon

severed, the dilemmas of class, taste
burgeoning in signs of stars   once traced,

their atlas   equipped the trappings
of a small dream, of a bird in flight, of tomorrow

constrained. every message, spreading
(wings, a wave without breath,

the starlings too   crowded, darkness
enveloping   a limit, of speech

*

considered, bloomed   the rotting heap, lifting,
a blanket of youth, of clouds, of every

the light somewhat, filthy
a crashing each heard   distinctly.

could its revelations   so risen
in watchtowers of yore, the neon burnt

if smoke, if the answer   if the question
positioned   a terrarium, the lives,

of those within,   who left behind,
the vase   which had carried, an ocean

a river, a little town

what they were carrying, in a post-industrial.
could its dream have seen it, could it have dreamed its airs,
what they would be carrying, post-industrially.

had it been shared, that dream, could it have been seen,
in the love of a little town, in the pride of a love of a little town.
what they were carrying in a little town,

what they were loving. in a post-industrial, the growth
of a little town, where it was going / growing
in a dream that was dreaming, in a post-industrial, the love

of a little town, of the little people, that made this possible.
could its dream have seen it, what it was loving,
could its plant have been growing, steadily, inside them.

had it dreamed its excess, had it dreamed its post-industrial.
what they were carrying, inside of its dream
the future was, a contamination, that was a future.

what was a future, in a contamination, what dream,
were they carrying into that future.
when they were loving a contaminated future, when it was

a cancer in a dream, that was carrying itself toward.
did they dream its airs, when it was growing, did they dream
its growing. they were loving the sound of a river,

of a river flowing through, the love of a little town.
was it patriotic, to suffer, was it patriotic to carry, was it patriotic
to dream. the sound of a river in the middle, of a little town.

they were loving, post-industrial, the dream of a river
in a little town, the sound of a river in a dream of a little town.
had it been growing, steadily, had it been among

those undreamt. what was outside the dream of the dream,
where a love of a river in a little town was flowing, where it
was flowing to, where it was being borne, in another future.

a sighting

a narrative would surrender suddenly
impressed, in unended layers—

could return in given scenic, indices
spread toward its touch— that several were

tissues worn, alighting.
had it circumstance, to disturb

that it was suddenly the whiteness
that it was hurtled, a grace

that it was wandering. had it been perfectly given
perfectly surrounded, the discharge,

what re-sounded. had it burned, as it leapt
the fire they were tending. its glance,

carried nothing from it as it leapt—
the speech it thought better of,

an arresting resonance, that razed,
its ideal of where.

how it planted the road, the destination
that had not been, received kindly.

*

un-earthed, what seraphim remained.
the birds that had been, had been

slaughtered, elegized in the patterns
of navigation, of its imperial dream,

a tracing, of the broken noise
which erupted. from its foundations,

none proclaimed a history,
none lacking what had been

forgotten, none moving
in the shadow-halls. which discontinued.

the one that had been speaking,
the many. where the flickering leapt

into the blueness one thought, collapsing.
had it sustenance, in its dismemberment,

had it opened into a small window
lit with vacancy. the distortions

of what was calling out, un-formed
torn from meaning, torn from its eyes.

Among the fields

perpetual i of its erasure, where another.
when in the dark.
when they were becoming, original
aboriginal
had the symphony broken down.
nothing could have been further from,
rediscovering discovery.
in a field.
that was alphabetizing
alpha, the aleph
when it was homogenous.
would it open, into different darknesses.

§

it could not situate, to ask
a question that was wanting there.
there were no, interruptions.
eruptions.
things that could never be falling.
never acquired.
things that could never be not acquired.
the bells, the bell tower.
the bells, the bell tower.
when the expedition set out, if speaking.
never an arrangement.
when / where never fallen.

§

the closed rank, concealed
its inception, what bridged beyond it
from within it.
again it would arrive, and again.
each time destroying nothing—
where the beginnings of its dream
arose in separations.
reparations.
she turned toward him, among the fields.
what lifted away from there
in its representations.
she turned away from him, among the fields.

§

nothing more gruesome contained
anything fuller than
what had been replaced,
superseded.
the architecture of it;
coming down, the vortext of vision
all hail, block letters
belles lettres, in its anti-bellum
nomenclature.
human nature, legislature.
this could not be photographed.
do you mind if we ask you some questions.

§

there could not have been, a "situation—"
while nothing allowed history.
as they were turning into crystal / flowers.
the dance that had been breaking,
(in) the duration of mimicry
the laurels crying—
where things were being salvaged,
savaged, out among the cries,
the echo of those who had not been
descried so lovingly.
as though a life, a crystal slowly.
where the day had become encrypted.

§

that they were collateral,
and lovingly willing. an insurance policy
that was gathering, in the clouds
that were remaking everything, slowly.
lowly, the most holy.
the time that had been posited
as use value, the usefulness they were
loving willingly.
in banners that spread and spread.
in anthems caught in the wind,
caught in the throat,
where reasons, were not necessary.

§

the broken cars played.
in the mind of the broken biosphere.
where the broken cars were playing,
in the severance pay
that had filled up its "territory."
its "biosphere" was not hermeneutic,
hermetic, when Hermes had been.
later, the broken mercury.
had it been more like a holiday.
in the choice that had not.
with its potential / ideal
somewhat reacting / leaching forward.

§

granules flared, (rocket's red)
without redness, what suspended a name.
in an otherwise euphoric.
phantasmagoric. euphonic.
that the death-in-life had been reversed,
where the reversal remained
unclosed, sonic, the redness of it.
when it had been superseded.
as though a tangible wish,
an assembly line of imaginary tulips / ships
filled with a defunct language.
the 1,001st word, and so on.

§

one that was red that was crying
in the aftermath
where the fallout, the fallout shelter
had driven away.
where the drawing up / drawing out was named.
they had been trained.
where one that was red that was
crying out, had mistaken.
its position(s).
although nothing more could fit, on the map.
had the excavation.
it was saying itself, as it was dis-locating.

§

in my catacombs, the complete implosion
where birds slung outside perception,
where they perched.
in perches that had been clung in flux,
where so Heraclitan.
as though the Titans had reversed / reserved fate.
and birds that flung forward, flung into my eye.
o my catacombs, that collapsed its love.
such that flight could not depart.
had there been the ease of a glance, then.
in that interim of speech.
again in the rain, the coming of the train.

O, polis

a fascination

in its virtual city   a mass, of voices   tangling with ghosts
they invoked, an after-image   reviving

its image, a horizon   that was disappearing   in its transmission,
a public broadcast   that forecast   'fear god

and the stupidity of the populace'   nebulous, they subsumed
that the dream of a benevolent father, that the *ex nihilo*

sweltered   *de facto,* that is now   and ever shall be
what overlay, the standard issue   which consumed what,

had there been   its permanent revolution, its permanent eulogy
that its 'inner life,' that its inner circle   one could look

to the mountains, with versions of clouds   where the traffic,
the trafficking, a spectacle   united, a state,   of illusory equality

under the banners   it processed in Mexico   dreaming each
in its own neon, its own   promenade   in the destruction

'pick up your china doll,' 'pick up your china doll,' pick up your
china doll,'   *ad hoc-ed,* could its meaning   carrying

the stamp   of communication,   the unraveling of the boulevard
as it recombined   a phantasmagoria,   its exhaust, feedback

a passing / a spreading

its act   of disappearance followed   another demonstration
its public space   receding in indistinct   patchwork

an ossification of formulae   larvae   if longing could
they dreamed of networks   inter-connectivity   four sparrows

dotting his wiring   what message   decoded sounded
sunrise sunrise in permanence   sunrise sunrise   as beginning

how the common ground   advanced its logic   how clearly
the wall distorts   an enveloping   one could not forget

what phantasy rummaging through   a version of history
a compression chamber   automated   auto-autonomous

could its i   upon awaking suggest   an alternative window
where the street   ended where   its image / images awaited

the ground   of a negativity   pulsating through its fabric
its certified documentation   a superhighway   full of exits

it could not negate   anymore it could not   suggest / infer its text
the incompleteness   of its residues   its unearthed cacophonies

when they were killing its animal.
when perhaps he should have. done something else.
while they were, the question.
remained. open.
perhaps he should have done something
else.
other its open. remained.
while they were away, killing, killing, killing—
while it was 'being killed off.'
where. other, than
the question of which. remained.
had it been done. had it been done. had it been done.
when they were killing its animal.
were they. away.
open.
have you met them.
when, perhaps, then, you should have done so.
they were killing its animal.
i was being 'thinned out'—
had it been done.
now it is the kind of dreamt that always did it.
had it been done.
while they had been watching,
what they were looking for.

*

so minimal, its animal.
infinitesimal.
a decimal, a decibel.
a crucible.
there were so many, on its Crusade.
along the way—killing, killing, killing
could it have loved terror.
could it have been named, Terror.
else, it claimed.
had they been thinking, something else.
it claimed. perhaps it should not have been.
altogether, unthought.
perhaps they should have
done something else.
have you spoken to them.
although it was not unheard.
it was being painted. over and over and over
again. could it not
come. would it not, again
come killing its animal. and weren't they,
if they could/if they couldn't.
in what kind of Dream, were they coming.
when did it run.

a market

were the heirlooms   agreed, upon were
the spirits packaged, in   weather, neighborhoods

tongued into   each other, identity caressed
what the consciousness said it answered

the burning   of its dream, this type of fire
in the absent,   foundation   could its reach

how it thought itself, how it said it answered
one spoke,   a knowledge,   an application of

they did not recognize each other,   skin was
everywhere   reincarnation was, everywhere

the radical could not see its variable, a closet of frost in its metaphysical winter, that the age of innocence somewhat too. continually, the ravishment, the rapture, its nature / nurture. what became popular, what development, which nomenclature which institutionalization. that its human-ism, appropriated, called out: yes / hosanna / hello, yes / hosanna / hello, a mirror pressed against the vortex. of the landscape stretching / receding into its eye, a collage of reason followed. that the footsteps, near dawn, could no longer be traced, that the traces were no longer replicating. suspended in a consumable virtue, the values of tradition, its mythological precedent. he became a flower that history lifted, from underneath the rubble, underneath its ink. how the whir of its vortex, lost its frequency, later the call of yes / hosanna / hello, the limit of intelligibility, the coarseness of its fiber. her longing, antiquated, abandoned itself, amidst the broken ships, the burnt out cities.

a wholeness, i answered

of a new garden they dreamed its winter, everything electric, kinetic, he was walking through it, where she followed, where she went.   only the language, unsorted, lifted in a wind that brought nothing, the absence of gardens he was walking, where she followed, where she went.   that the signified could not lighten, that neither were carrying it.   an impossible dance enmeshed the lights, the lenses, where its winter expanded, where it fell away.   that the fallen world, was not theirs, that the voices each carried, tangled in the spaces they opened, where a sun could have been.   only everything, was infinite, he could no longer, celebrate its landscape, she could no longer, include a sprinkling of stars, the ledge of morning.   that the risen world, was not theirs, she was walking, where he followed, where he went.   an impossible music lifted, a further music, one that returned, with the absence of music.   the ends of dream narratives spread out into the blankness, words, letters dissociating, vestiges of themselves, they were walking where it followed, where it went. everything insubstantial, potential, each to be written again, to be dreamed again, each one disappearing together.

Where a road had been

> *"Love re-presents I to itself broken (and this is not a representation). It presents this to it: he, this subject, was touched, broken into, in his subjectivity, and he is from then on, for the time of love, opened by this slice, broken or fractured . . ."*
>
> —Jean-Luc Nancy, "Shattered Love"

someone that history forgot that forgetting so positively.
a positively someone that disappearing
mattered most recently.
where its name went,
where it arrived.
should it have been 'made,'
should it have been 'constructed,'
were Plato etc. to blame.
instead, should, say, someone so positive,
someone so identified,
someone so fully.
what it could not remember what could not be remembered.
where was it looking,
and with / at whom.
the present does not / did not ask questions.
about someone so positively there could not be asked,
someone so forgotten,
so disappearing.
who was it, that thought to ask:
as it departed it could not impart.

§

completely, severally, properties stretched.

a unification a myth.

'people' so distinct, so contrasted.

as it contrasted, so fully, there were logics / residuals.

as it considered, (so considerate)

it became, mechanized.

the future did not / does not whisper.

its ghosts so sated.

that it was punctured, punctuated

that words were leaking,

into its landscape.

what was peripheral was anything peripheral was everything peripheral.

who, concerned, mentioned its dimensions.

nobody was keeping score.

there 'one' said 'we' without noticing.

on a plane so flat, so treated.

its weather.

overlooking it,

looking back at it,

that it had not made suggestions / impressions.

§

nothing could be emptied of.

one so timely could be emptying when it was beginning.

nearly nearly leaving it was nearly there.

where it had presence / presences.

that one so timely considered moving forward / not moving.

where it neared what it was nearing,

where it was. considered. (considerate.)

had it lamented justly.

one so justly speaking.

'people' in thinking of other 'people.'

a landscape emptying the 'landscape'

where they had been speaking.

one heard it lightly, positively.

the essence of it,

the essences of it,

its 'essential nature.'

it was splitting it so positively so completely.

if it were separating,

if it were unifying.

they were all asking: what they were overlooking.

§

what they were trying to do,
when they were moving toward.
that it was always collapsing.
could they positively.
it might reiterate what could have been happening,
it might just reiterate.
could they all fit inside of it.
who was crossing,
who was so self-possessed,
so timely.
what they were spilling when they were building.
what they were drilling, along with building.
so many were filling,
so many were filling out.
it was 'making room,' for its substitutions.
were they a' waiting, in those wings, (trilling) were they.
some things were written,
'others' were written about.
where everything answered / was answering everything else.
utility is a pitiless god.

§

did it linger its nation.

did it ascertain, it was completely civil,

when it was in order, when was it in order.

they were thinking: 'it is completely civil,'

it was completely entertained.

from it sprang, (it sprang from) caricatures,

shades they were springing.

it had been outlined,

it was blurring.

everything was running / reuniting from.

from it sprang equivocations / (it sprang from) where,

two sides were meeting.

where two sides were meeting they were talking of meeting / reuniting.

that it was justified in.

there were concerns,

that it was behind everything.

holding it up, to the light.

it could have been reiterated / returned.

that it could have been something else,

that there were 'others' there.

§

no one was calling out to everyone else.

what no one said when it called, the space it used.

how the sounds resembled,

a type of music,

how the music suggested,

a kind of finale.

they were humming along, measures of harmony.

that they had been, breeding,

an apocalypse.

that its 'wait here' surrounded.

that it was pushing through.

fabric, skin, the text that each might have been,

the coloration of.

a certain eternity.

it's tablecloths, it's linens.

the firmament which upheld, what upheld its firmament.

they were humming along, a measured harmony.

a road, a tree, a cloudless sky.

they were patrolling, the border(s),

that alienation might yet blossom, fruitful.

§

a road, drenched in sky, the houses of a road, its meanings.
that it implicated, its viewer.
that its viewer was viewing,
something already viewed.
that the parameters were altering.
a road drenched in sky, the houses of a road, its meanings.
the city / country, urban / rural of its spent,
its infusion.
where investment,
where it could have been.
a road, drenched in sky, the houses of a road, its meanings.
given its placement, its signature(s),
looping through / into whiteness.
where whiteness, a sighted dream,
a cited road,
a site of insurance / assurance.
the regulations leaching, toward / away
(from) kingdoms of things.
in general, the natural, a processing of process.
a road, drenched in sky, the houses of a road, its meanings.

§

what the picture could be, what it knew.
where it could have been,
what was, excluded.
a perceiver shouldered, what it was thinking of.
it held its eye, they held their gaze,
it was not static.
when the sequence believed / contaminated.
when the frame became, unauthorized.
that a quintessential American, a quintessential pastoral.
what was pushing, against the skyline.
when it claimed, its difference.
something coming through it, clearly.
one so cleanly speaking,
others so cleanly listening.
what was agreed upon.
this too began.
could it 'hold forth,' could it 'come to terms.'
could / did its material resolve / dissolve.
was it always, already an ideal.
what they were / were they holding on to.

§

anything loves a something particularly.

practically anyone loves them all.

each one, a full of possibilities,

each one, a plethora of recourse / resource.

practically anyone is an everyone,

even a someone particularly.

particularly everyone, doubly singular, a multiply multiple.

a multiple of kind, a kind of likeness.

a like of kindness. what liked an unlike,

it was certainly saying something.

what disliked,

what it disliked,

what was it like.

what it liked it loved, were it a who.

practically a particular love, a particulate view, a new.

were it a view, were it empty of who.

was it certainly saying something.

was it reminded of,

what was it reminded of,

was it reminding / remaining.

§

so blank, a blanketing of.
that it might have returned, had it.
what was walking, through / with.
where it became blanker,
could it have been an every one, an every I even.
the marks it was making, hollowing out.
as it thought, its world.
nothing filling with trees, suggestions of wind, the burnt edges, thumbed.
it was still moving, the possibilities of rivers.
a blanketing of rivers.
the sky unechoed.
where a road had been, with its inflections.
could its edge remain an edge, could it.
intact, an edge, a question, a tongue.
the tension of a bird they were watching,
as an arrow somewhat, unmoving.
its marginalia.
had it already been resolved, a mirror of sorts.
elsewhere, a cloud ringing mountains.
in its distance, the typing of rain.

§

had we seen something different / differently.
a distinct inking, had it pressed,
linking.
an inkling, the things a hand might do / say.
were we touching.
that its 'avant garde' had a 'how to' manual.
with certain pieces of sky.
on surfaces, which might have reflected / refracted.
a circumstance / circumference.
light was, salvation,
a stillness, a miniature, an eternity.
where its writing occurred,
what it was writing about / around.
they had been 'just leaving' for a while.
that time was all around, transcending.
were leaving, a kind of loving.
if / that its 'position,' was / were always changing.
had it taken, action.
they were asking, were we touching,
was it full, of signatures, was it.

§

did they love what they were loving.
when they were loving it.
that it could have been, had it.
that it clearly, nearly was. was it so each, so distinct.
that it discarded, a selection of clouds.
so natural, it had been easily.
eliminating everything, it was determined.
there were determinations, definitely.
so easily differing definitely,
so nearly purely.
so surely.
they could not see, what was coming.
an event, that had been coming, partially eventually.
impartially, elevated, the notes of dictation.
that there was a code.
although it had been, loosely defined, definitely.
what had been deferred, so deferential.
they became defensive.
they were knowing, and knowing how / what they had been.
that they were all knowing: and knowingly known.

§

i could not cover, where it was / (where was it) going.
i could not dis-cover.
that anything might have occurred.
that occurring, a version of snow, a blanket of reason.
had it been speaking, of windows.
had it clearly, wintered.
it had been dealing, with information / with which information.
had it been dealing with informations.
were informations informative, were they in-forming.
what was in, what was forming.
the type was telling.
the type of in-formation, that was telling.
that form, too, would always, fall,
a kind of snowing.
a kind of wind, that was wrapping.
had it a forest.
could they have weathered it.
where dis-covery was becoming.
in a fledgling sky,
with a destructible wing.

§

nothing could be ended evenly.
if they were clipped,
if they trailed sentences, colors.
were it nearing what it had been claiming.
upon which palette, had it sufficed.
in the meantime, had the situation been changed.
what they were driving through it,
how it changed, the shape of it,
how it altered itself, evenly.
that its sylvan historian, suggested otherwise.
that they were dedicated, among otherwises.
which otherwise would which.
would which remember itself as other,
as a meaning, as a leaving.
it seemed the dirge, the trodden, what had already begun.
they were reaching (for) each other,
into / among the borderlands.
when it began stopping, un-meaning:
when it was catalogued,
were its dream so delightful, so dreamy.

§

to be or not to be, that is its answer.

it was representing,

what it was representing, that representation, an in-forming of craft.

and were they sailing / stalling.

that it was nearly time,

that it was nearly a time,

that it was currently, and passing.

and were they sailing along, and was it confessing something.

to whom is a home,

they were always renovating,

innovating the innovated, and innovatively so.

was it an ovation, that was being born(e),

could it be a birth and was it a wave / a sailing.

long, so long, along the horizon,

long, so long, along the horizon,

what might have been, inside a line, how it was opening.

and were they really assailed / a wave.

if it had a curtain,

if it had a balcony.

had it believed, in a horizon, in that kind of caress.

§

it was so dirty, it was fucking.

they didn't want its nakedness, its exposition.

it could not be subtle, they were only waiting, in a smaller distraction.

what it might have called / what it might have called out.

and what for.

were they thinking, its audience, were they.

it was so dirty,

it was loving,

it was a kind of curtain.

that there was a panorama, a vision of outside,

something wished,

something sailing.

had it been a window, a castle.

a partition, a patrician, a crest of noise.

in its exposition, an exposing.

that it was always covering up.

that they were always covering up.

what they were saying, and so baroque.

from the window, a fluted baroque, a meant firmament.

and could they see its façade, could they.

§

a rising of hounds, could a howl still.

once placed, the extent, of its damage.

was it 'in the distance.'

he was 'replaying it,'

that it 'had to be repeated,'

when it 'had to be spoken.'

it had to deliver, what it had to deliver upon.

could a howl, still breathe, at its reach, at its river.

and where was it opening / its opening.

that a clearing, streamed,

that its sounds were placing / replacing.

what was, once, itself.

what was receiving and was it also howling.

must it have been abandoned,

and was it fading / fading away.

how were they feeling, about their perceptions.

and what could be brought, to them.

were they 'in the distance,'

were they smeared / smudged,

what was flowing, against its textures / its grains.

§

its heart, always open / broken.
opening / breaking away from it-self.
that its self was opening itself open.
although where, its captivating, its conclusion.
could it be opening / breaking, summarily, could it be its continually.
its open / broken, always heart, hurt.
a dis-heartening crest, so fallen,
what it was picking up.
what was being received.
at its reception, nothings were leaving, a part of something, each.
an opening / broken plane,
a field of which.
that its heart was opening its heart was.
and where, they were loving.
and where it-self opening / breaking,
that its opening, un-open.
as if it were spoken, leaving.
as if it were leaving, it-self behind.
a part of something, not-beyond, un-returning,
a heart opening / closing / breaking.

Matt Shears was born and raised in northeast Ohio. He graduated from the University of Iowa Writers Workshop and was a Schaeffer Fellow at the University of Nevada-Las Vegas. He currently lives in Oakland, California, with his wife and daughter and their three cats. *Where a road had been* is his first book.

Made in the USA
Monee, IL
07 July 2026

56552442R00042